Ripley's Believe It or Not!

Developed and produced by Ripley Publishing Ltd

This edition published and distributed by:
Mason Crest Publishers Inc.
370 Reed Road, Broomall, Pennsylvania 19008
(866) MCP-BOOK (toll free)
www.masoncrest.com

Ripley's Believe it or Not!
Extraordinary Endeavors
ISBN 978-1-4222-2018-4 (hardcover)
ISBN 978-1-4222-2052-8 (paperback)

Library of Congress Cataloging-in-Publication data is available

Ripley's Believe it or Not!—Complete 16 Title Series
ISBN 978-1-4222-2014-6

1st printing
10 9 8 7 6 5 4 3 2 1

Library of Congress Cataloging-in-Publication Data is available.
Printed in USA

PUBLISHER'S NOTE
While every effort has been made to verify the accuracy of the entries in this book, the Publisher's cannot be held responsible for any errors contained in the work. They would be glad to receive any information from readers.

WARNING
Some of the stunts and activities in this book are undertaken by experts and should not be attempted by anyone without adequate training and supervision.

Believe It or Not!®

The Remarkable... Revealed

Mason Crest Publishers

EXTRAORDINARY ENDEAVORS

Staggering successes. These fantastic feats

and mind-boggling adventures will have you

gasping in utter amazement. Read about people

who can lift 100 lbs (50 kg) using their teeth, walk

on raw eggs without breaking them, and wear

121 t-shirts all at the same time.

It took Canadian Kyle Macdonald exactly
one year to turn a red paperclip into a house...

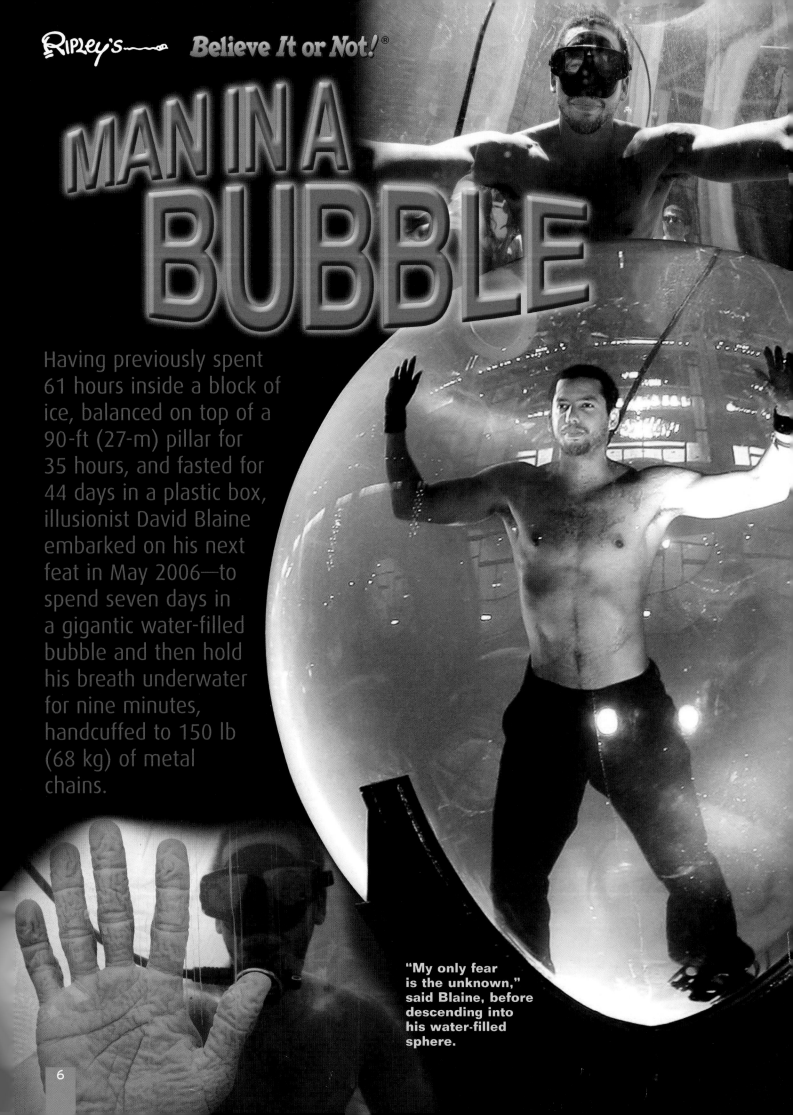

MAN IN A BUBBLE

Having previously spent 61 hours inside a block of ice, balanced on top of a 90-ft (27-m) pillar for 35 hours, and fasted for 44 days in a plastic box, illusionist David Blaine embarked on his next feat in May 2006—to spend seven days in a gigantic water-filled bubble and then hold his breath underwater for nine minutes, handcuffed to 150 lb (68 kg) of metal chains.

"My only fear is the unknown," said Blaine, before descending into his water-filled sphere.

Blaine said afterward that the ordeal in the big goldfish bowl was "horrific in many, many ways. Every muscle doesn't just ache, it feels like a sharp, shooting pain—like a knife being stabbed."

keep him alive, and the water inside his "human aquarium" was maintained at around 97°F (36°C). He said he would try to sleep whenever possible during the week-long performance.

But the final challenge proved beyond Blaine. Two minutes short of his nine-minute goal, after appearing to release his hands successfully, he began struggling to free his feet from the chains and divers had to pull him from the water. Looking shaken and weak, and his skin peeling, he thanked his supporters and headed straight for hospital where doctors tested his physical health. Prolonged submersion in water brings with it a number of hazards, including nerve damage and blackouts, but Blaine's main complaint was a feeling of skin pain "like constant pins and needles."

Blaine prepared for the stunt by training with U.S. Navy Seals and shedding 50 lb (23 kg) in body weight over the previous few months to improve the efficiency with which his body used oxygen. In the week before the challenge, he practiced holding his breath and refrained from eating any solid foods so that he wouldn't need the bathroom while inside the 8-ft (2.4-m) acrylic sphere.

Hundreds of people turned out to see Blaine lowered into the tank at the Lincoln Center for the Performing Arts in New York City, wearing pants, rubber shoes, and a special diving mask. Tubes fed him oxygen and liquid nutrition to

This was a challenge too far for Blaine, who confessed: "I've never felt this kind of pain in a stunt."

CUTTING EDGE

American magician Matthew J. Cassiere (also known as Matt the Knife) is a skilled fire-eater. He can escape from a pair of handcuffs in five seconds and has escaped from a straitjacket in under 19 seconds.

STUNT KID

In July 2006, 12-year-old Australian motorcyclist Tyrone Gilks landed a jump of 169 ft (51.5 m) on his 85cc bike during a celebration in Butte, Montana, honoring U.S. stunt legend Evel Knievel.

KAYAK MARATHON

In May 2006, 34-year-old Brandon Nelson kayaked more than 146 mi (235 km) in 24 hours on a 2-mi (3-km) course near Lakewood, Washington State. On the way, he battled strong winds, broke his custom-made boat, and had to paddle a slower boat for over 5½ hours until his was repaired.

HIGH MILEAGE

Irvin Gordon of Long Island, New York, has driven more than 2.5 million mi (4,023,360 km) in his 1966 Volvo car!

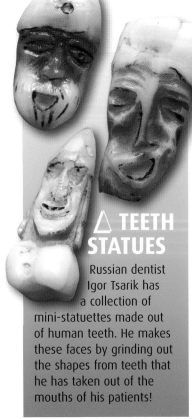

△ TEETH STATUES

Russian dentist Igor Tsarik has a collection of mini-statuettes made out of human teeth. He makes these faces by grinding out the shapes from teeth that he has taken out of the mouths of his patients!

HANG UPS ▽

Johnnie Reick was able to eat and drink while hanging upside down for 1 hour 57½ minutes in Ocean Park, California, in 1930.

△ BALANCING ACT

In 1934, Robert Ripley himself asked a contact in India to look for performers who might come to the U.S.A. to appear at his Chicago Odditorium (a museum), and this is one of the photographs he received.

BASE JUMPER

Thrill-seeker Roger Holmes rode a mountain bike off cliffs 360 ft (110 m) high in Sussex, England, in 2006—and survived. Holmes, a 37-year-old BASE jumper, was in freefall for two seconds before opening his parachute and landing on the beach 12 seconds later. The term "BASE" jumping is an acronym of the objects jumped from—building, antenna, span (bridge), and earth—and Holmes has completed more than 250 jumps in ten countries.

YOUNG BUCK

John Jordan "Buck" O'Neil, who died in October 2006, played in a minor-league baseball game in July 2006—at the age of 94! He had signed a one-day contract to play for the Kansas City T-Bones, the first time he had swung a bat in a game since 1955. A former player and coach, O'Neil said afterwards: "I've been in baseball 70 years—this is how I made my living. And here I am at 94 with a bat in my hand!"

STRANGE JOURNEY

In 2006, Roz Gordon traveled the length of Britain using 73 different types of transport! The 35-year-old landscape photographer from Suffolk took six weeks to make the 1,162-mi (1,870-km) trip from John O'Groats in Scotland to Land's End, Cornwall, England, in 183 stages. Her modes of transport included dog sled, pogo stick, hoppity hop, camel, unicycle, go-kart, ambulance, catamaran, lawn mower, golf cart, canoe, luggage cart, paddle boat, quad bike, skateboard, tricycle, rickshaw, wheelbarrow, and stilts. She used each method for at least 328 ft (100 m) and a maximum of 50 mi (80 km) and finished the journey with a piggyback from her brother Phil.

STRING STUNT ▽

A Chinese stuntman pulls a rope out of his nose that has passed through his mouth, into his throat, and through his nasal passages.

TIGHT FIT

Wu Xizi, a Chinese contortionist, squeezes his 67⅜-in (1.71-m) frame into a box measuring 23⅝ in (60 cm) long, 11¾ in (30 cm) wide, and 15¾ in (40 cm) high in Nanjing in eastern China on May 22, 2006.

SEVEN UP!

By reaching the top of Mount Everest in 2005, Danielle Fisher had climbed the highest peaks on all seven continents. And she was still only 20! The Washington State University student, who is 5 ft 7 in (1.7 m) high and weighs 130 lb (59 kg), started climbing at the age of 15 when her father took her to climb Mount Baker in northwest Washington. She began the Seven Summits circuit in January 2003 by scaling Mount Aconcagua in Argentina, following that up with Mount Kilimanjaro in Tanzania, Mount Elbrus on the Russia–Georgia border, Mount Kosciusko in Australia, Mount McKinley in Alaska, Mount Vinson Massif in Antarctica, and finally Mount Everest.

JUNIOR SCIENTIST

Maya Kaczorowski of Hamilton, Ontario, Canada, wrote a research paper on headaches caused by ice cream. When she was only 13 years old it was published in the *British Medical Journal*!

◁ REVERSE RUNNING

Swiss runner Rinaldo Inäbnit, 28, was the proud winner of a 7-mi (11-km) run in the Swiss Alps in 2006, but, unusually, he ran the distance backwards. The new sport of "retro-running" is gathering pace in several European countries, with athletes retraining their brains to accommodate their back-to-front coordination. Inäbnit won the race with the aid of a rearview mirror, and told reporters afterwards that his motto is: "Don't look back in anger. We have to move forward backwards."

CROSS-COUNTRY RIDE

A group of about 30 cyclists completed an eight-week cross-country ride from Providence, Rhode Island, to Seattle, Washington, in August 2006 to raise funds for affordable housing. They averaged about 75 mi (121 km) a day on the grueling 3,800-mi (6,115-km) westward journey.

DEEP DIVE

In the Red Sea in 2005, Nuno Gomes, a 53-year-old civil engineer from Johannesburg, South Africa, made a scuba dive to a depth of 1,044 ft (318 m), which is the same height as the Eiffel Tower, including the aerial on top. "I went very close to what was physically impossible," he said. "I knew that I couldn't go another meter deeper. If I'd gone any deeper, it would have meant my death."

SWEET TOOTH ▷

Gamini Wasantha Kumara, 39, from Sri Lanka, lifts one of the fifty 110-lb (50-kg) bags of sugar that he picked up with his teeth during a competition in the capital, Colombo, in 1999. The same strong set of teeth were earlier employed to pull a 220-ton train.

ECONOMY DRIVE

In 2006, John and Helen Taylor of Melbourne, Australia, drove a Volkswagen Golf 18,100 mi (29,129 km) around the world in just 78 days and on less than 24 tanks of fuel. They attributed their achievement to their "relaxed and measured" driving styles.

GREAT ESCAPES

Chicago escape artist and magician Thomas Solomon has escaped from maximum security jails in the U.S.A. and the U.K., from a locked, burglar-proof, titanium steel bank safe under 30 ft (9 m) of water, and from a 20-lb (9-kg) ball and chain at the bottom of the Hudson River. He has also escaped from more than 1,000 pairs of handcuffs and various types of straitjacket.

PANDA ▷ PORTRAIT

Using a single rabbit hair as a paintbrush, Jin Yin Hua took ten days to create a picture of a giant panda on a strand of human hair. His artwork is so tiny that visitors to the Chinese gallery where it was on display had to view it through a microscope. The New York micro-painter also creates portraits of people on single strands of hair. He has carved portraits of the King of Brunei and silent movie star Charlie Chaplin on lengths of white hair.

MINI MONSTER

British rally champion Stefan Attart has given his Smart forfun² vehicle an upgrade, transforming it into an impressive all-terrain 4WD. The chassis has been jacked up to 145 in (368 cm), supported by 26-in (66-cm) wheel rims with a diameter of 55 in (140 cm), achieving a total vehicle height of 12 ft (3.7 m). A massive six-cylinder diesel 5,675cc engine provides the necessary oomph.

SENTIMENTAL JOURNEY

In 2005, British artist Shelley Jacobs embarked on a journey to visit all 288 streets in the U.K. bearing the name "Shelley." She traveled thousands of miles to photograph the signs, and plans to expand her quest to other countries.

NEVER TOO OLD

Edward Nelson of Jacksonville, Florida, aged 67, does pull-ups with a 45-lb (20-kg) plate tied to his waist.

◁ HORNED MAN

Kung Fu practitioner Wang Ying from Jiangsu province, China, discovered a tumor the size of a rice grain on his forehead in 1991, at the age of 59. Fourteen years later, the tumor had grown to almost 2 in (5 cm) in length and measured just over an inch (3 cm) in diameter, and Wang Ying was able to lift 14 bricks with it!

MONSTER DRIVE

Wade Goldberg can drive a golf ball 411 yards (376 m)—and he's only 17. The East Texas teenager produced his monster drive—longer than four football fields—at a junior long driving competition in 2006.

BIRTHDAY JUMP

To celebrate her 90th birthday, Britain's Mary Armstrong chose to jump out of a plane at 12,000 ft (3,660 m). The great-grandmother of nine made her first parachute jump when she was 87 and hopes to be doing it when she is 100.

BLIND FAITH

South African Hein Wagner completed a 24-mi (40-km) cycle race in 2006—even though he is blind. By following a friend with a noise-making device attached to the back of his bicycle, Wagner finished the arduous Construction du Cap Ninety Niner race around Durbanville in under two hours.

△ PLAYING THE HIGH NOTES

Conservationists cleaning the U.K.'s highest mountain in May 2006 were astounded to find a piano weighing 226 lb (103 kg) on the summit! And it turned out that the piano had been on the 4,409-ft-high (1,344-m) Ben Nevis in Scotland for 35 years, having been carried there by strongman Kenny Campbell in 1971.

LEGLESS HERO

A New Zealander who lost both legs to frostbite climbed to the top of Mount Everest in 2006. Mark Inglis, 47, reached the summit of the world's highest mountain in 40 days even though one of his carbon legs broke during the climb and he had to repair it. Fortunately, he had taken a spare set of limbs and parts in case of an accident. Inglis had lost his real legs below the knees when he was trapped by a storm while climbing New Zealand's highest peak, Mount Cook, in 1982.

Fast Food Eaters

MANGO MUNCH
The only rule of entry for the mango-eating contest is an ability to eat 6 lb 10 oz (3 kg) of mangoes in 3 minutes!

WINGING IT
Competitors in Philadelphia, Pennsylvania's 2005 buffalo-wing eating contest ate up to 10 lb (4.5 kg) at a sitting!

PIG'S FAT SNACK
At the salo-eating contest in the Ukraine, competitor Volodymur Stregalin ate 2.2 lb (1 kg) of pig's fat!

SHRIMP SUPPER
The winner of the seafood-eating contest in China in August 2005 gobbled up 18 meaty mantis shrimps.

WATERMELON EATERS
Whoever manages to swallow the greatest amount of watermelon in a set time wins this eating contest held in the Chinese city of Zhengzhou.

CORNED BEEF AND CABBAGE
Ed "Cookie" Jarvis of New York won a contest by eating 6 lb (2.7 kg) of the combo in 10 minutes.

COLLECTIONS

WHEELCHAIR THRILLS

Tyler Deith of Muskoka, Ontario, Canada, goes to extremes in his quest for thrills—even though he has been confined to a wheelchair since a motorcycle accident in 2002. He once traveled at 50 mph (80 km/h) in his wheelchair while hanging on to the back of a friend's car and has also hung on to the back of moving buses. By way of a change, he rides skateboard ramps on his manual wheelchair, performing a variety of daring stunts.

CRACKING FINALE

For the closing show at the 2006 Pyrotechnics Guild International Convention near Kaukauna, Wisconsin, Dave Carlson pushed a button to detonate 9.8 million firecrackers!

KAYAK KAREN

Karen Richardson of Florida traveled 1,750 mi (2,816 km) to Nashuam, New Hampshire, by paddling a kayak.

WALKING ON EGGSHELLS ▷

In 2005, Zhang Xingquan from northeast China's Jilin province not only managed to pull along a family car using his ear, but achieved his astonishing feat while walking on clutches of raw eggs, only one of which appears to have broken!

CONCORDE TUG

British strongman Dave Gauder once pulled a 101-ton Concorde aircraft a distance of 40 ft (12 m) along the runway at Heathrow Airport, London. He also held back two Piper Cherokee 180 aircraft, one with each arm, to prevent them taking off, and on another occasion he lifted a Volvo estate car weighing 4,180 lb (1,896 kg) off all four wheels.

EYELASH LIFTER

Ashok Verma of Agra, India, can lift heavy objects—using only his eyelashes. He has lifted three 50 fl oz (1.5 l) bottles of Coca Cola with a string attached to his eyelashes and says he can lift an 80-lb (36-kg) stone by the same method. His ultimate goal is to pull a car using his eyelashes.

FLYING JCB

The usual function of a JCB engine is powering a lumbering mechanical digger, but in August 2006 a turbocharged version of the same thing propelled a racing car to speeds of over 350 mph (563 km/h) at Bonneville Salt Flats, Utah. The British JCB Dieselmax, driven by Wing Commander Andy Green, has six gears and reaches 110 mph (177 km/h) in first. It shifts into third gear at 270 mph (435 km/h) and is fitted with a parachute to help it slow down.

BALL JUGGLER

An 11-year-old Hungarian boy, Bence Kollar, juggled a soccer ball an impressive 2,214 times in a Budapest bar in 2006 without the ball once touching the ground.

△ CRAZY CAR WRECK

Passersby in a street in Berlin, Germany, were surprised to see this unusual arrangement of cars in July 2005. No, it wasn't a funky art installation, but was the unfortunate result of driving without due care and attention. The yellow VW Beetle drove into the back of the Audi—a move which somehow resulted in the Audi ending up on top of the Beetle!

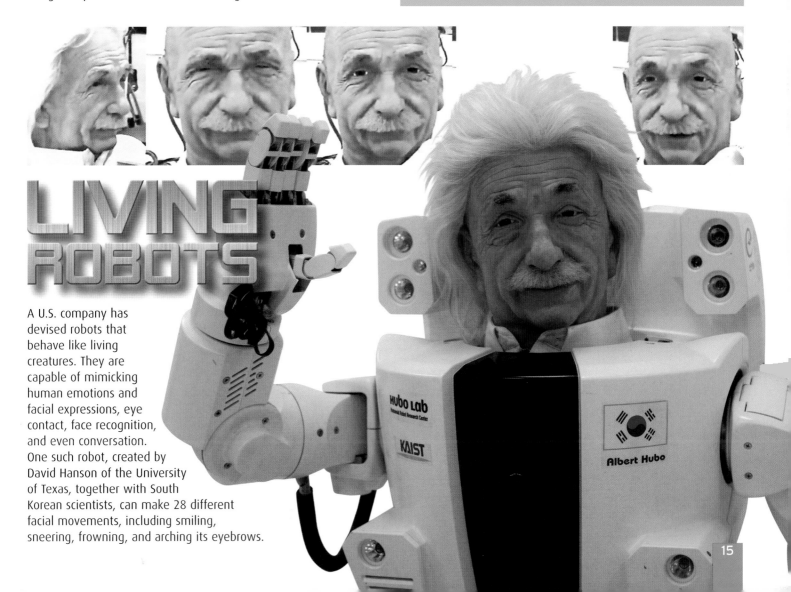

LIVING ROBOTS

A U.S. company has devised robots that behave like living creatures. They are capable of mimicking human emotions and facial expressions, eye contact, face recognition, and even conversation. One such robot, created by David Hanson of the University of Texas, together with South Korean scientists, can make 28 different facial movements, including smiling, sneering, frowning, and arching its eyebrows.

15

BIKE RIDE

Gary Eagan traveled 5,632 mi (9,064 km) from Alaska to Florida by motorcycle in 101 hours, setting a new record certified by the "Iron Butt Association."

BRIDGE JUMPER

In July 2006, Oregon National Guard captain Dan Schilling made 201 BASE jumps in 24 hours off a bridge 486 ft (148 m) above the Snake River Canyon near Twin Falls, Idaho. And the 43-year-old kept jumping even after fracturing his wrist. The feat required the assistance of 15 parachute packers and 25 other personnel, and Schilling admitted: "The difference between life and death on every jump is about two seconds."

FAIR CROSSING

Linda Fair crossed Canada from coast to coast over a period of four years using a dog team and a customized adult-sized tricycle.

FREE FORMATION

A total of 400 skydivers from 31 countries held hands to shape a spectacular midair free-fall formation over Thailand in February 2006.

WOMAN CAGED

A 25-year-old Chinese woman spent a week living in a cage with 300 birds in the spring of 2006. The cage, suspended 12 ft (3.7 m) above the ground, was equipped with a bed and a computer. The woman said she hoped to increase her awareness of conservation by experiencing a caged bird's pain.

OUTRAN TRAIN

Despite having to navigate heavy morning traffic along the 1.5-mi (2.4-km) highway, marathon runner Steve Moneghetti outran a commuter train in Sydney, Australia, in June 2006!

WATER BALLOON FIGHT △

In April 2006, a crowd of 2,921 people launched a staggering 55,000 water balloons at each other during a massive water fight that took place on a beach in Sydney, Australia.

COURAGEOUS CLIMBER

Despite being paralyzed in a mountain climbing accident, Mark Wellman of Truckee, California, has made ascents of the sheer granite faces of El Capitan and Half Dome in Yosemite National Park. A talented wheelchair athlete, he was also the first paraplegic to sit-ski unassisted across the Sierra Nevada Mountain Range.

BOWLED OVER

In June 2006, 40-year-old Dave Wilson of Mason, Ohio, bowled continuously for 102 hours—a period of four days and nights.

EPIC WALK

Canadian Jean Béliveau is partway through his epic 12-year walk around the world, covering 47,224 mi (76,000 km). The former neon-sign salesman set off from Montreal on August 18, 2000. Traveling alone with a three-wheeled stroller containing food, clothing, a first aid kit, a small tent, and a sleeping bag, he walked through North America to South America before crossing the Atlantic to South Africa and then walking up to Europe. By August 2006 he had reached Britain. The remainder of his journey will take him through the Middle East, Asia, Australia, New Zealand, and finally back to Canada by 2012. His accommodation has varied from using the tent, staying with friendly families, or sleeping at local police stations and churches. His wife Luce visits him every Christmas... wherever he is in the world.

YOUNG KICKER

Laudon Wilson of Herrin, Illinois, could kick field goals over regulation goal posts at the age of three!

◁ BALEARICS SWIMMER

Spanish long-distance swimmer David Meca arrives at San Antonio, Ibiza, on January 5, 2006, after a 21½-hour nonstop crossing from the Spanish mainland town of Javea—a 64-mile (110-km) odyssey, during which he overcame bouts of vomiting and swarms of jellyfish.

Airbed Spectacular

The waters off Coogee Beach in Sydney, Australia, were the venue in 2006 for a lineup of 863 hot-pink airbeds, all in the shape of giant flip-flops! The event took place on Australia Day (January 26), and flip-flops were chosen as the shape of the airbeds in homage to their status as an Australian fashion staple. In addition, participants maneuvered the enormous line of airbeds to form an outline of Australia.

Ripley's—

STEEL BAR
Steel bar bent by John Brookfield of Pinehurst, North Carolina, with his bare hands.

KARATE DEMOLITION

Fifteen members of the Aurora Karate Club in Ontario, Canada, demolished an entire house in 3 hours 6 minutes 50 seconds!

SKATEBOARD TREK

In August 2006, two months after skateboarding the length of Britain—some 900 mi (1,448 km)—Welshman Dave Cornwaithe set off for an even more daunting challenge—to skateboard 3,000 mi (4,828 km) across Australia. The 27-year-old graphic designer's trek from Perth in Western Australia to Brisbane, Queensland, on the country's east coast took him across hundreds of miles of scorching desert and lasted 90 days. Arriving in Brisbane in January 2007, he said that he'd mostly skated early in the day because it was far too hot during the day to do anything.

MINI MARVEL ▽

Lu Di won admiration at a kung fu school in Songhshan, China, in July 2006 by performing 10,000 push-ups in 3 hours 20 minutes. But what really astounded onlookers was the fact that he was just six years old! The school's president, Shi Yongdi, was so impressed that he decided to waive the boy's tuition fees for the next ten years.

HAIR-RAISING FEAT

Chinese artist Tseng Hai Sun and his partner Brigit enjoy a cup of tea above the harbor in Hamburg, Germany, while hanging from a crane hook by their hair. They were promoting their circus show, which featured the ancient Chinese art of braid hanging—exponents of which were hung by their hair to demonstrate courage.

KEEP FIT

At age 91, Ervin Ashley of Springfield, Oregon, climbed 2,000 steps every day, five days a week, to keep in shape!

TABLE TOPPERS

Sharon Linter, Lorraine Jones, Steve Hammond, and Rhian Jones played nonstop table soccer in aid of a charity for the homeless for an impressive 33 hours 35 minutes at Swansea, Wales, in 2006.

TEENAGE PILOT

Inglewood, California, resident Jonathan Strickland is already an accomplished pilot—even though he is only 14. In June 2006, Jonathan, who has been training to fly since 2003, was flown to Canada, where youngsters can obtain a pilot's licence at 14, compared to 16 in the U.S.A. There, he achieved the unique distinction for someone his age of flying solo both an airplane and a helicopter on the same day.

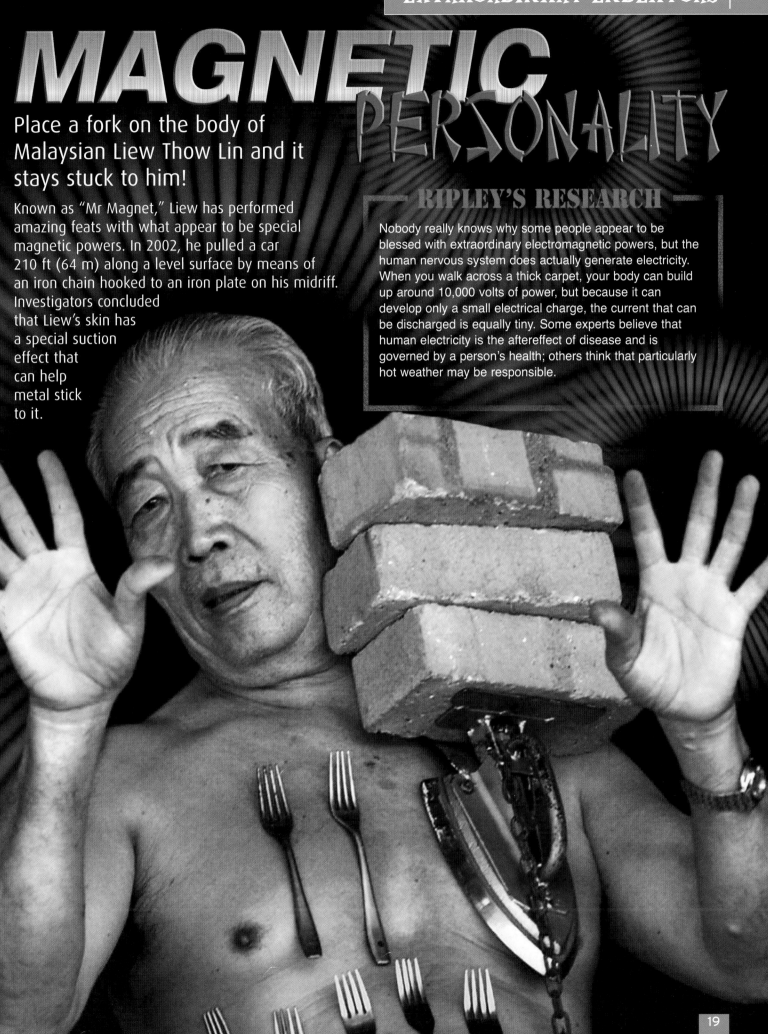

MAGNETIC
PERSONALITY

Place a fork on the body of Malaysian Liew Thow Lin and it stays stuck to him!

Known as "Mr Magnet," Liew has performed amazing feats with what appear to be special magnetic powers. In 2002, he pulled a car 210 ft (64 m) along a level surface by means of an iron chain hooked to an iron plate on his midriff. Investigators concluded that Liew's skin has a special suction effect that can help metal stick to it.

RIPLEY'S RESEARCH

Nobody really knows why some people appear to be blessed with extraordinary electromagnetic powers, but the human nervous system does actually generate electricity. When you walk across a thick carpet, your body can build up around 10,000 volts of power, but because it can develop only a small electrical charge, the current that can be discharged is equally tiny. Some experts believe that human electricity is the aftereffect of disease and is governed by a person's health; others think that particularly hot weather may be responsible.

PHIL THE FLIPPER

Show Phil Pfister a car and the chances are he will want to flip it over! For Pfister, born in Charleston, West Virginia, is 6 ft 6 in (2 m) tall, weighs 325-lb (147-kg), and has been named the strongest man in the U.S.A., so flipping cars or pulling two huge 18-wheelers comes naturally.

PULLING TEETH

In summer 2006, Wang Xiaobei, a 72-year-old Chinese grandmother, pulled a four-ton truck, loaded with people, for more than 30 ft (10 m)— with her teeth! In the winter of 2005, Wang had pulled two cars, also with her teeth.

ROAMING PIGEON

When Judy the homing pigeon set off from Bourges, France, on July 7, 2006, she was expected to fly the 596 mi (959 m) back to her owner John Stewart in Northumberland, England, in 48 hours. But she never made it home. Instead, seven weeks later she turned up 5,000 mi (8,047 km) away on the Caribbean island of St. Eustatius in the Dutch Antilles! It is thought that she was blown off course and hitched a ride on a passing ship.

HELICOPTER LIFT ▽

Strongman Franz Muellner from Austria lifted a 4,000-lb (1,800-kg) helicopter on his shoulders for almost a minute at the 2006 Vienna Prater, a famous funfair held each summer between March and October in the Austrian capital.

FIRE-EATER

When his eldest brother suffered serious burns, George McArthur of Bakersfield, California, overcame his fear of fire by eating it! He is a regular fire-eater on the sideshow circuit, where he also swallows swords and devours insects. And at 7 ft 3 in (2.2 m), he lives up to his nickname "The Giant."

SNOW WONDER

Austrian army officer Josef Resnik, 52, skied the Schorshi piste for 240 consecutive hours over ten days in the winter of 2005, taking only short breaks to go to the bathroom, eat, and have a warm shower.

DESERT JUMP

Jumping from a ramp 39 ft (12 m) long and 10 ft (3 m) high, 24-year-old Nathan Rennie cleared over 121 ft (37 m) on his mountain bike in the Painted Desert, South Australia, in November 2005.

NATIONWIDE READ

On August 24, 2006, more than 150,000 students right across the U.S.A. read the same book on the same day. The literary event attracted more than 1,200 groups, meeting everywhere from schools to coffeehouses to read the 77-year-old classic *The Little Engine That Could* about a small locomotive that struggles to gets its train over a daunting hill.

FAIR CHALLENGE

Grover and Gamet Castro of Stow, Ohio, have visited every County Fair in the state of Ohio—that's 88 fairs!

AUTOGRAPH HUNTERS

Akram Marufshonow and Musadshon Chornidow, two soccer fans from Uzbekistan, cycled 4,000 mi (6,437 km) across Europe for three months in 2006 to get the autograph of their favorite player—German national team goalkeeper Oliver Kahn.

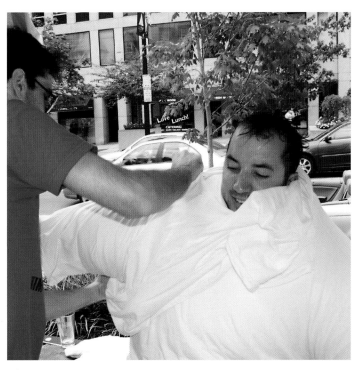

△ TRIAL BY T-SHIRT

David Alexander got a little hot under the collar in 2006, when he put on an incredible 121 T-shirts one on top of another. His friend, Will Sharp, spent almost two hours helping David into the garments, which ranged in size from small to 8XL. Despite sweating profusely in the 93°F (34°C) heat, by the end of the exercise David tipped the scales at 285 lb (130 kg), 75 lb (34 kg) over and above his usual weight.

PAINTERLY ▷ SWIM

Italian painter and long-distance swimmer Alberto Cristini has combined his two passions in life to create the art of "swim painting." Since 1997, Cristini has swum acoss lakes, bays, and seas around the world, including Lake Garda and the Strait of Messina in Italy, English Bay in Vancouver, British Columbia, Canada, and San Francisco Bay, California, painting all the while on a specially created floating easel, which he guides with his right hand and paints on with his left. Cristini says: "I tried to make a fusion between what I do, so I invented swim painting."

BACKPACK RUN

With a heavy 40-lb (18-kg) backpack strapped to his back, U.S. soldier Jake Truex of Albany, Oregon, ran 5,468 yd (5,000 m) in just 22 minutes 20 seconds in Hanau, Germany, in February 2006.

SKATING AWAY ▽

Peggy Gray spent a lot of time walking or roller skating upside down near her home in Plainfield, New Jersey, in the 1920s and 30s.

MECHANICAL MARVEL

In 2006, a British mechanic was still working full-time—at the age of 100. Buster Martin actually retired at 97, but three months later he applied for the job maintaining a fleet of plumbing vans because he found retirement boring.

MOBILE THROWER

Finland's Lassi Etelatalo won the gold medal at the 2006 Mobile Phone Throwing World Championships by hurling a scrapped Nokia unit nearly 300 ft (91 m). Around 100 throwers from as far afield as Canada, Russia, and Belgium converged on the competition held in Finland.

Unrattled

On November 9, 2006, American Jackie Bibby, alias "The Texas Snakeman," held a frightening ten western diamondback rattlesnakes 2½ ft (76 cm) long in his mouth for 12.5 seconds!

BIKERS' BURNOUT

By scorching their rear tires simultaneously, more than 260 motorcycle riders staged a mass burnout at Maryville, Tennessee, in August 2006. The bikers performed the burnout by locking their front brakes, gunning the throttle, releasing the clutch and letting the rear tire spin against the asphalt.

DOUBLE BACKFLIP

Riding up a ramp, 23-year-old Travis Pastrana of Annapolis, Maryland, soared into the air on his 200-lb (90-kg) motorcycle and made two complete revolutions to land a double backflip at the 2006 X Games—the first time such a stunt had been performed successfully in X Games competition.

TREE PLANTING

In an attempt to improve air quality in the Philippines, volunteers simultaneously planted more than 500,000 trees on 2,137 mi (3,439 km) of road across the archipelago on August 25, 2006.

AMPUTEE PILOT

Despite suffering 40 per cent third-degree burns and losing his left leg in a 1989 fighter aircraft accident, Commander Uday K. Sondhi of the Indian Navy has retrained as a helicopter pilot. To date, he has flown nearly 2,000 hours.

EVEREST LANDING

In 75 mph (121 km/h) winds, Frenchman Didier Delsalle touched a helicopter down on the summit of Mount Everest in 2005. To make it even more hazardous, Delsalle had no idea whether he was landing on snow-covered rock or merely a lump of brittle ice, which would have instantly given way beneath the helicopter.

TRACTOR TREK

In 2006, a group of 15 vintage tractors, each with a top speed of 30 mph (48 km/h), crossed the width of Australia from Perth, Western Australia, to Cape York, Queensland—that's an epic journey of more than 3,400 mi (5,472 km).

BLIND TEAM

The Seeing Ice Dogs are a hockey team located in Calgary, Canada. The team is so named in honor of the fact that the majority of the players are blind. They use a metal puck with ball bearings inside so that they can follow its sound.

OVERCAME PAIN

In January 2005, a British escape artist who calls himself David Straitjacket escaped from a special high-security straitjacket in Manchester, England. The jacket had loops and buckles designed to be inoperable from inside the jacket, but David managed to extract himself from it in 81.24 seconds, dislocating his right shoulder in the process!

BIKE JUMP

In October 2005, motorcycle stuntman Ryan Capes of Seattle, Washington, became the first person to jump more than 300 ft (91 m) on a bike when he leaped a colossal 310 ft 4 in (95 m). At Ohio Bike Week in June 2006, Capes achieved another landmark jump when he cleared 120 Harley-Davidson bikes. Ramp-to-ramp, this jump measured 187 ft (67 m).

BALANCING ACT ▽

Jewgenij Kuschnow maintains his balance in a headstand for 15 minutes on the roof of a moving car. The journey took place in Munich, Germany, on November 5, 2006.

PRETTY AS A PICTURE ▽

A woman and two children walk in between a painting made by 800 children in Bucharest, Romania, on November 18, 2006. It stretched for an amazing 2.2 mi (3.6 km).

ONE MAN WENT TO MOW ▽

On July 4, 2006, Bobby Cleveland of Locust Grove, Georgia, roared along the Bonneville Salt Flats at a speed of more than 80 mph (130 km/h)... on a lawnmower! The eight-time National Lawnmower Racing Series champion, Cleveland built the specially modified mower from scratch over a period of six months.

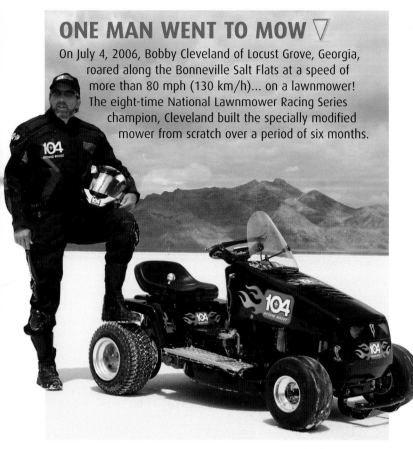

COAST TO COAST

In 2006, Ginny Bowman from Rochester, Vermont, teamed up with her 13-year-old son and two of her teenage nieces to cycle across the U.S.A. from California on the west coast to Connecticut in the northeast to raise money for diabetes research. Despite facing temperatures of up to 118°F (47.8°C) and several arduous mountain climbs, they managed to cover an average of 65 mi (105 km) every day.

STEP CLIMB

Medical student Jonathan Hague climbed the 242 steps of Australian landmark Jacob's Ladder no less than 269 times in the space of 24 hours in 2006. Climbing the Perth beauty spot 215 times equates to climbing the height of Mount Everest.

INDIA WALK

In an incredible feat of endurance, Sabalsinh Vala of Toronto, Ontario, Canada, walked 6,200 mi (9,978 km) across India.

YEARLY DIP

Between 1928 and 2003, Ivy Granstrom of Vancouver, British Columbia, Canada, took a swim in the ocean near English Bay every year on New Year's Day—that's 76 years running!

SKI FANATIC

When he swept down Oregon's Timberline ski area on July 27, 2006, Rainer Hertrich reached the milestone of 1,000 consecutive days of skiing. Since November 1, 2003, Hertrich, from Boulder, Colorado, skied somewhere every day, clocking up 34 million vertical feet (10,363,200 m) in the process. On an average day, he skied 33,000 vertical feet (10,058 m)—that's higher than Mount Everest. He battled through cold, frostbite, rain, and illness, and once hiked up an active volcano in Chile because it had more snow to ski down than neighboring mountains!

GREAT ADVENTURER

Singapore's Khoo Swee Chiow is one of the world's great adventurers. He has scaled Mount Everest twice, climbed a 26,335-ft (8,027-m) peak in Tibet without any oxygen, skied to both the North and South Poles, broken SCUBA diving records, cycled from Singapore to Beijing, and climbed the highest peaks in seven continents.

VETERAN PILOT

Jonas Blanton of Battle Creek, Michigan, is a daredevil glider pilot—even at the age of 84. Blanton has specialized in aerial stunts for more than 60 years and in June 2006, at Whitewater, Wisconsin, he piloted a glider that was towed by a small plane to an altitude of 11,050 ft (3,368 m).

MUSIC DEGREE

Tammie Willis of Richmond, Virginia, received a master's degree in music from Virginia Commonwealth University—the first deaf student ever to earn a music degree there.

SUPERIOR CROSSING

Although he nearly drowned as a child and didn't learn to swim until his late twenties, Jim Dreyer of Grand Rapids, Michigan, is now one of the world's foremost endurance swimmers. In 2005, towing a supply dinghy, he completed a 60-hour solo swim across Lake Superior, battling storms, 15-ft (4.6-m) swells, and powerful rip currents that pushed him off course and increased the distance of his swim from 55-mi (89-km) to 70 mi (113 km). His success meant that he had finally achieved his goal of swimming all five Great Lakes.

WHEELCHAIR STUNT

Trevair Snowden of Gardnerville, Nevada, performs daring stunts in a gas-powered wheelchair. Trevair, who has been in a wheelchair since breaking his back in a snowboarding accident in 1997, races his four-wheeler up a 5-ft (1.5-m) ramp, vaults through the air, lands on a flaming rail, and travels 12 ft (3.6 m) down it on the slide plate—a piece of metal at the bottom of his vehicle. He describes himself as being "like Evel Knievel in a wheelchair."

ALPINE GIFT

Keizo Miura of Japan celebrated his 99th birthday by skiing down the 12,600-ft (3,840-m) high Mont Blanc along with his 70-year-old son Yuichiro.

CARRIAGE PULL

In 2006, a man worried about reaching the age of 60 pulled a carriage 430 mi (692 km) across Hungary in a bid to prove he was still as strong as when he was younger. Fifty-nine-year-old Laszlo Aranyi dragged the 924-lb (419-kg) carriage from Zahony, on the country's eastern border, to Szombathely in the west in 22 days.

DOUBLE ACE

A golfer playing in a weekend tournament at Lubbock, Texas, in July 2006 followed up his first-ever hole in one with another one—on the same hole and using the same club. What's more, Danny Leake, a 53-year-old insurance agent with a 14 handicap, aced the sixth hole with a five-iron on consecutive days.

NET BUSTER

Tom Waite reeled in no fewer than 42 trout in seven minutes while fishing at the State Fair Park in Milwaukee, Wisconsin, in 2006. That means he caught a fish approximately every ten seconds.

MAKING A SPLASH

Swiss businessman Frank Rinderknecht sped across the English Channel in 3 hours 14 minutes in July 2006, in his amphibious sports car "Splash." The car's innovative design enabled it to skim across the surface of the water, but the choppy waters of the world's busiest shipping lane still made the crossing a pretty bumpy ride.

INTERNET TRADER

Aged 27, it took Canadian Kyle MacDonald just one year to turn a red paperclip into a house of his own on Main Street, Kipling in Saskatchewan— simply by making 14 trades over the Internet.

Starting with a simple online offer on July 12, 2005, two women from Vancouver snapped up the big red paper clip in exchange for a wooden fish pen that one of them had found on a camping trip. MacDonald made swift progress until followers of his adventure despaired when he traded an afternoon with rock star Alice Cooper for a snow globe featuring the band Kiss. But MacDonald knew that Hollywood director Corbin Bernsen was an avid snow globe collector and, sure enough, Bernsen was happy to add the globe to his 6,500-strong collection, in return offering MacDonald a role in his next movie *Donna on Demand*. Finally, the town of Kipling offered to trade a 1920s house for the movie role, which it planned to auction off to promote the area.

fish pen

doorknob

camping stove

electric generator

neon beer sign

snowmobile

Where did you get the idea from?

"From the children's game "bigger and better." I created a website for the project, and promised to visit potential traders wherever they were— I traded for a pen in Vancouver, a doorknob in Seattle, even a movie role in Hollywood."

Why did you start with a red paperclip—and did you always have a house as your goal?

"It was the first thing I saw when I thought of the idea in my apartment in Montreal. We were renting, and wanted to own a house—it was kind of a joke, but also I figured there didn't have to be an upper limit."

Did you think you'd become a global internet phenomenon?

"No! At first people just thought I was freeloading! I travel all around the country as a trade show representative, so I would make the trades as I went—and gradually more and more people started reading my blog, from as far away as Japan."

How did you finally get your house?

"Director Corbin Bernsen had offered me a speaking part in a film he is writing and directing. He has a collection of 6,500 snow globes, and when I found one featuring the band Kiss, I knew I had something to offer him in return. I then traded the movie role with the town of Kipling, which held auditions for the part."

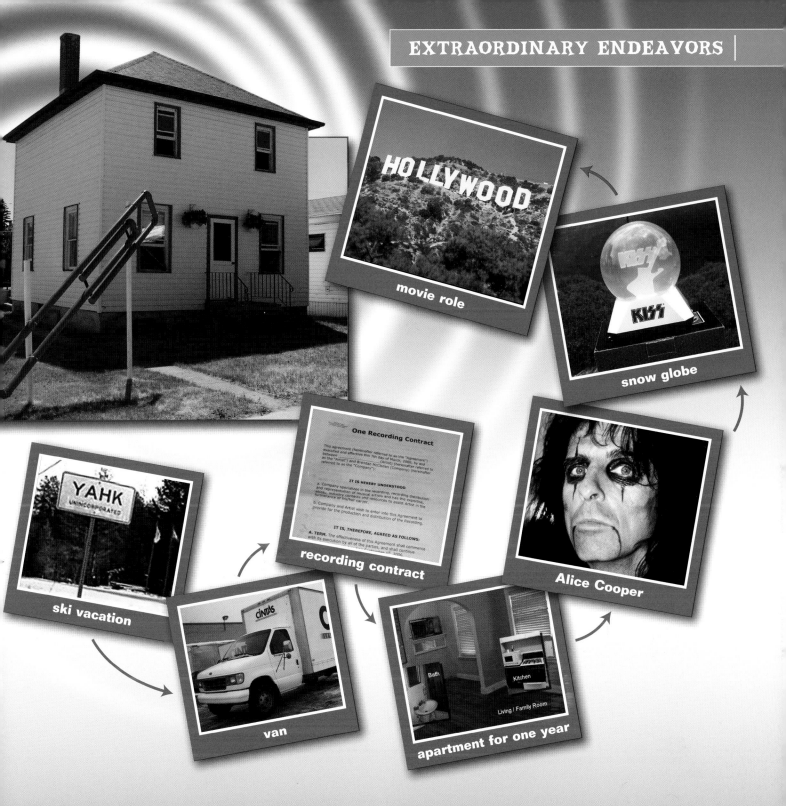

movie role

snow globe

recording contract

Alice Cooper

ski vacation

van

apartment for one year

Who got the role?

"A local guy called Nolan Hubbard will be in the film *Donna on Demand*—he just blew the crowd away. He was more than ecstatic to get it. He works at a local recycling depot."

What was your favorite trade—and which was the riskiest?

"My favorite was the first trade, the red paperclip for the fish-shaped pen, because if I hadn't made that one, nothing else would have happened. People thought trading an afternoon with Alice Cooper for a snow globe was risky, but I knew I had the trade with Corbin lined up—I left it a week before making the trade to see what people would think, though—they freaked!"

Were you ever worried it wouldn't work?

"I was anxious every step of the way. It was stressful—the phone was ringing 20 times a day with people calling from all over the world. I stopped eating and sleeping and regular things like that!"

What will you do next?

"I'm writing a book about it all. I don't think I'll be trading again just yet—even for a 'bigger and better' wedding day!"

How did you celebrate getting your house?

"We had Saskatchewan's biggest housewarming party ever—several thousand people came to Kipling, which only has a population of 1,140. They're going to put the world's largest paperclip—a giant red one—at the entrance to the town. And I proposed to my girlfriend Dominique—we are getting married next summer."

SURE TOUCH

Carl Celella of North Greenbush, New York, can easily find any of the 70,000 items in the plumbing department he manages for Home Depot—despite being completely blind.

NOTTINGHAM QUEST

Alex Picker from the city of Nottingham, England, embarked on a six-week trip in 2006 to visit 14 other Nottinghams around the world. He began with Nottingham, in Saskatchewan, Canada, and then visited 11 Nottinghams in the U.S.A.—two each in Alabama, Ohio, and Pennsylvania, and one each in Virginia, Maryland, New Jersey, New Hampshire, and Indiana. Then he flew to South Africa where he paid a visit to the Nottingham Road Village. He also called in on two Nottinghams in Scotland, although both turned out to be just farms.

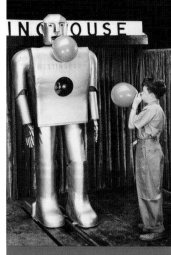

ROBOT BREATH

This robot, built by U.S. firm Westinghouse in 1932, was able to inflate a balloon with its mouth. Westinghouse later created breathing apparatus machines, of which this may have been the forerunner.

SPEED CYCLIST

"Fast" Freddy Markham has designed a bicycle that can travel in excess of 50 mph (80 km/h) over a sustained period of time. The former Olympic cyclist from Soquel, California, covered more than 53 mi (85 km) in one hour at a special challenge in July 2006 in his recumbent bicycle, Easy Racer, and won $18,000 in prize money as a result.

MASS DRIBBLE

More than 1,000 students dribbled basketballs simultaneously at a college in Bendigo, Australia, in 2006. A total of 1,111 people took part, the biggest problem being to find enough balls for them all!

HUDSON SWIM

On July 28, 2004, Christopher Swain of Portland, Oregon, became the first person to swim the 315-mi (507-km) Hudson River. It took him eight weeks to complete the swim.

WING WALKER

An 85-year-old Englishman has developed an unlikely interest— wing walking on an airplane! Grandad Tom Lackey of Solihull, Warwickshire, took up the sport in 2000 following the death of his wife and in 2006 completed his 14th wing-walk when he was strapped to the upper wing of a biplane as it performed a loop and a roll 2,000 ft (610 m) above ground.

GIANT CABBAGE

A gardener from County Durham, England, grew a cabbage almost as tall as him! Frank Watson's prize spring cabbage was 5 ft (1.5 m) tall, 16 ft (4.9 m) round and had more than 100 leaves.

DARING DIVE

Scuba divers Mark Brimble and Jan Burt from the Aloha Dive Center in Limassol, Cyprus, spent 24 hours underwater in 2006 without coming up for any surface breaks.

BULLET BIKE

In 2006, Ironman competitor Greg Kolodziejzyk of Calgary, Alberta, Canada, traveled 650 mi (1,046 km) in 24 hours on his bullet-shaped bicycle called Critical Power. Riding around the track at Eureka, California, he averaged more than 27 mph (43 km/h) on his two-wheeled recumbent bike and didn't get out of the vehicle once during the 24 hours.

CHARITY RIDE

A nine-year-old boy from Calgary, Alberta, Canada, completed a 205-mi (330-km) charity cycle ride to Edmonton over two days in August 2006. Noah Epp learned to ride a bicycle at the age of three and has been going on 10-mi (16-km) rides since he was six years old.

TWO ACES

Marva Ged of Boynton Beach, Florida, beat odds of 67 million to one by hitting two holes in one in a single round of golf.

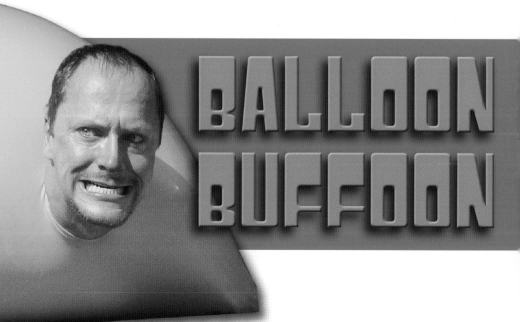

BALLOON BUFFOON

DIAMOND FORMATION

A team of 85 skydivers teamed up to form a giant diamond in the sky above Lake Wales, Florida, in November 2005. Dropped from an altitude of 24,000 ft (7,315 m), members of the canopy formation branch of skydiving (in which fliers team up to form geometric shapes in the air) quickly assumed their designated positions as their formation descended at a speed of 1,000 ft (300 m) a minute. The skydivers were able to secure themselves to each other by wrapping their feet around the lines of the parachute below them.

KITE CROSSING

Despite failing to cross the Antarctic by kite-powered buggy when he was becalmed by a lack of wind, Britain's Brian Cunningham refused to give up on his quest for adventure. In September 2004, joined by Kieron Bradley and Peter Ash, he crossed the hostile Gobi Desert in Mongolia in a kite buggy, traveling at speeds of 40 mph (64 km/h). The three men made the 625-mi (1,006-km) crossing in 17 days.

LONG MARRIAGE

In 2006, Bill and Eluned Jones of Slough, Berkshire, England, celebrated their 83rd wedding anniversary! Mr Jones was 105 and his wife was 102.

Danish clown Lars Lottrup performed his eye-catching act at the International Clown Festival in Copenhagen, Denmark, in August 2006. A crowd favorite, Lottrup manages to get himself sucked gradually into a giant orange balloon.

SITTING TARGET

Angelo del Monaco of West New York, New Jersey, allowed 128 motorcycles, each weighing up to 800 lb (363 kg), to run over his body in 2006. He lay on the pavement under a 150-lb (68-kg) board, while 13 bikes took turns running over him, one by one, for seven minutes. He said it was the most dangerous stunt he had ever done. "When you jump over cars, you have control. ... But I can do nothing here—my life depends on the motorcycle riders."

ONE-ARMED GOLFER

Ask golfer Lee Norton his handicap and he'll tell you straight: he can only play with one arm. But Norton, of Greeneville, Tennessee, can hit a golf ball farther with one arm than most people can hit it with two. He lost the use of his right arm in a motorcycle crash in 1987 but refused to be deterred from playing his favorite sport. And in August 2006 he drove a golf ball, one-armed, an amazing 296 yd (271 m).

FAST MOVER

Furniture mover and former wrestler James Clark of Edina, Minnesota, reeled off an incredible 751 push-ups in 30 minutes in August 2006.

STEP MASTER

Indianapolis fireman Jim Campbell climbed more than 106,000 steps on a step mill in 24 hours in August 2006. The feat is equivalent to completing a half-marathon vertically or climbing the steps of the Empire State Building 56 times.

TRICYCLE TREK

Dan Prince of Joseph, Oregon, traveled a distance of 4,250 mi (6,840 km) across the U.S.A. on a 27-speed tricycle to raise awareness of the benefits of gas-free travel.

SCUBA RELAY

Six men and a woman swam the English Channel in 2006 in an underwater SCUBA relay. The British team completed the 21-mi (34-km) journey from Dover, England, to Cap Gris Nez, France, in just over 12 hours. Their biggest worry was huge passenger ferries. Organizer Colin Osbourne said: "When you're under water, you don't know where they're coming from and you think, it's going to hit me!"

SHARP ART ▷

Monks from the Shaolin Temple in China's Henan province are famous for their combination of Zen Buddhism and martial arts. One of their "mind-over-matter" skills is shown here being exhibited at a martial arts show in the city of Xining in Qinghai province, China.

IN DEPTH
DIFFERENT STROKES

London-based long-distance swimmer Lewis Gordon Pugh has conquered the coldest and roughest stretches of water in the world. Known as the "Ice Bear," he can control his own body temperature to battle the elements.

What made you want to swim in extreme conditions?

"My father was an Admiral in the Royal Navy, and he used to read me stories about Captain Cook, Lord Nelson, and Captain Scott. When I was 10 we moved to South Africa and at 17 I had my first swimming lesson—one month later I swam the 7 km (4.3 mi) from Robben Island to Cape Town and barely made it."

You're the first person to complete long-distance swims in all five oceans of the world. What was your longest swim?

"The longest continuous one was the English Channel at 35 km (22 mi). The longest "staged" one, where I swim for a day, sleep, then carry on the next morning, was down the River Thames which was 350 km (217 mi)—I swam the equivalent of half the Channel each day for 21 days. At least the pleasure barges avoided me—but there were lots of jelly fish at the mouth of the river!"

Which were the most dangerous?

"Round the Cape of Good Hope because of the sharks, or inside Deception Island, a flooded volcano in the Southern Ocean. The temperature was 2°C (35°F) and I swam for 30 minutes—the longest Polar swim ever completed."

What are some of the worst obstacles you have encountered on a swim?

"My "big five" predators are the Great White shark, the hippopotamus, the crocodile, the polar bear, and the leopard seal. The least intimidating is actually the Great White—they can come along and look at you, and then speed off!"

How do you prepare for a swim?

"I train physically for power and endurance, but the battle is not in the arms, it's between the ears. I use techniques to turn all my doubt into certainty, so when I stand on the edge of an iceberg and prepare to dive in, I have no doubt that I will get to the other side."

Is it true you can control your body temperature?

"It's done subconsciously. I don't tell myself to start heating up—we believe it's a Pavlovian response to many years of cold swimming. I swim in just trunks, cap, and goggles—no wetsuits. I stand on the edge and look at the cold, and my core body temperature rises from 37°C (98.6°F) to 38.4°C (101.1°F), which is the difference between life and death."

Have you received any serious injuries on a swim?

"So far no. We watch for predators before a swim—I don't get in the water near a penguin because they are the diet of a leopard seal. We've also designed an anti-shark device, which creates a pulse around our boat."

How will you top your achievements so far?

"I never do the same swim twice—the next one has always got to be bigger, longer, harder, colder, rougher! And it has to be a first—I'm a pioneer swimmer. There is better to come!"

BIG MOUTH

Marco Hort from Switzerland stuffed an impressive 264 brightly colored drinking straws into his mouth, beating his earlier best of 259 straws, in Vienna, Austria, in 2006. Marco dislocates his jaw in a painful but necessary maneuver in order to achieve his feat.

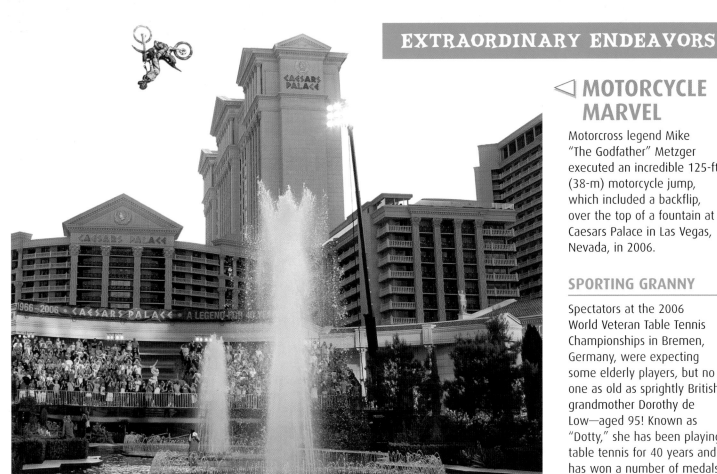

◁ MOTORCYCLE MARVEL

Motorcross legend Mike "The Godfather" Metzger executed an incredible 125-ft (38-m) motorcycle jump, which included a backflip, over the top of a fountain at Caesars Palace in Las Vegas, Nevada, in 2006.

SPORTING GRANNY

Spectators at the 2006 World Veteran Table Tennis Championships in Bremen, Germany, were expecting some elderly players, but no one as old as sprightly British grandmother Dorothy de Low—aged 95! Known as "Dotty," she has been playing table tennis for 40 years and has won a number of medals in seniors' competitions.

LOYAL EMPLOYEE

After more than 75 years working for public transit agencies, Arthur Winston retired from the Los Angeles Transportation Authority in March 2006—on his 100th birthday. In his entire career he missed only one day's work—in 1988 when his wife died.

PUZZLE EXPERT

Californian Leyan Lo solved a Rubik's Cube in 11.13 seconds in San Francisco, California, in January 2006. He has even solved the cube blindfolded in less than 1½ hours!

JET SKI JOURNEY

In June 2006, South Africans Adriaan Marais and Marinus Du Plessis set off on jet skis from Anchorage, Alaska, on a 13,000-mi (20,921-km) trip to Miami, Florida. Their route took them down the west coast of the U.S.A., then through the Panama Canal to the east coast. Three years earlier they made a 5,000-mi (8,047-km) jet ski trip along Africa's east coast.

MIRACLE ARROW

Anne Rohner of New Haven, Indiana, shot an arrow that pierced the brackets of an 8-ft (2.4-m) fluorescent tube and came to rest inside the light—all without breaking the glass exterior of the bulb!

CAUGHT SHARK

Melissa Ciolek, 15, of Orleans, Massachusetts, landed an 11-ft (3-m) blue shark, weighing 364 lb (165 kg), single-handedly in 40 minutes off Martha's Vineyard in 2006.

PUSH-UP KING

John Morrow of Ottumwa, Iowa, was sitting in a waiting room at the doctor's office when he read a magazine article about great feats of strength. He immediately set out to surpass those feats and in May 2006 completed an amazing 123 backward-hands push-ups (where the wrist is at a 90-degree angle) in one minute. Morrow says the key to his success is a 40-day fast that he takes each spring.

ACE AT LAST

After 77 years of playing golf, Vivian Barr of Vancouver, British Columbia, Canada, made her first-ever hole in one in 2006—aged 95! Barr, who is also a regular ten-pin bowler, hit her ace with a seven-iron on Point Grey's 114-yd (104-m) second hole.

TOWED TRAILERS

John Atkinson, aged 70, towed more than 100 trailers for nearly 328 ft (100 m) in Clifton, Queensland, Australia, in February 2006. He hitched his Mack prime mover up to 112 loaded trailers, with a total length of 4,837 ft (1,474 m).

△ LONG JOURNEY

This 1919 Studebaker touring car was driven an incredible 520,000 mi (836,859 km) in just 5½ years in the early 1920s. For part of this time it was owned by a transit company and was driven 400 mi (645 km) daily on routes in California.

Index

ACKNOWLEDGMENTS

COVER (t/l) Giovanni Zardinoni www.studioartezj.net, (b/l) www.goldeagle.com, (t/r) Courtesy of David Hanson, (b/r) Sandy Maxwell/John Muir Trust. The John Muir Trust acquired Ben Nevis Estate which includes Britain's highest point at Ben Nevis summit (1334m) in June 2000. www.jmt.org; 4 Courtesy of Kyle MacDonald; 6 (t, c) Reuters/Brendan McDermid, (b) Reuters/Mike Segar; 7 (t, b) Reuters/Brendan McDermid; 8 (t) Sobchenko Grigory/Itar-Tass/UPPA/Photoshot; 9 (l) Reuters/Sean Yong, (r) Reuters/China Daily China Daily Information Corp—CDIC; 10 (c) Urs Flueeler/epa/Corbis, (b/r) AFP Photo Sena Vidanagama; 11 (t/c, t/r) PA Photos, (b) Rex Features; 12 (fc, t) Sandy Maxwell/John Muir Trust. The John Muir Trust acquired Ben Nevis Estate which includes Britain's highest point at Ben Nevis summit (1334m) in June 2000. www.jmt.org, (b) Chinafoto Press/Camera Press; 13 (t/l) Reuters/Gleb Garanich, (b/l) Reuters/China Daily China Daily Information Corp—CDIC, (b/c) Stephen Chernin/Getty Images, (b/r) Reuters/Stringer Shanghai, (c/r) William Thomas Cain/Getty Images, (t/r) Reuters/Adnan Abidi; 14 Newscom; 15 (t) Newscom, (c, b) Courtesy of David Hanson; 16 (b) Reuters/Gustau Nacarino, (t) Ian Waldie/Getty Images; 17 Ian Waldie/Getty Images; 18 (t/r) Kay Nietfeld/AFP/Getty images, (b) Reuters/China Daily China Daily Information Corp – CDIC; 19 Reuters/Bazuki Muhammad; 20 Vladimir Kmet/AFP/Getty Images; 21 (t) Newscom, (b) Giovanni Zardinoni www.studioartezj.net; 22 (sp) Timothy A. Clary/AFP/Getty Images; 23 (b) Reuters/Bogdan Cristel, (t) Reuters/Alexandra Beier; 24–25 (b) Newscom, (t) www.goldeagle.com; 25 (t/l) Courtesy of Trevor Andre Snowden; 26–27 All courtesy of Kyle MacDonald except Alice Cooper—Live Press Agency/Rex Features, and town sign—www.cooperphoto.ca; 28 (b) PA Photos; 29 PA Photos; 30 Oliver Chouchana/Gamma/Camera Press; 31 (bgd) Terje Eggum, (t) Investec Asset Management, (b) Terje Eggum; 32 (bgd) Marc Chesneau/Fotolia.com, PA Photos; 33 (t) Ethan Miller/Getty Images

All other photos are from Corel, PhotoDisc, Digital Vision and Ripley's Entertainment Inc.